IL: LG
BL: 6.9
Pts: 0.5

HOW PEOPLE IMMIGRATE

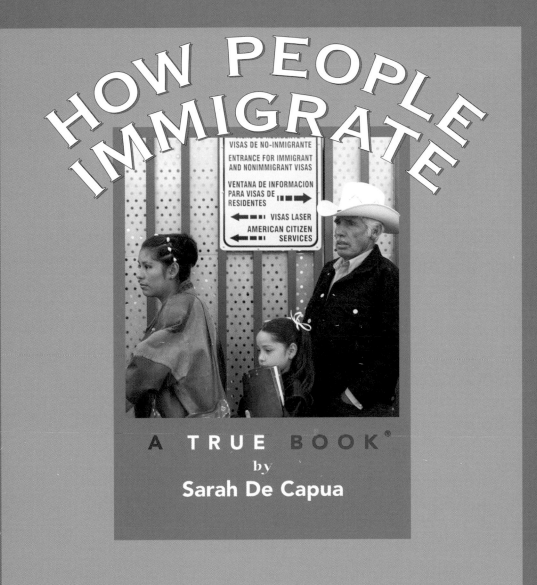

VISAS DE NO-INMIGRANTE

ENTRANCE FOR IMMIGRANT
AND NONIMMIGRANT VISAS

VENTANA DE INFORMACION
PARA VISAS DE ➡➡➡
RESIDENTES

⬅⬅⬅ VISAS LASER

AMERICAN CITIZEN
⬅⬅⬅ SERVICES

A TRUE BOOK®

by

Sarah De Capua

Children's Press®

A Division of Scholastic Inc.

New York Toronto London Auckland Sydney
Mexico City New Delhi Hong Kong
Danbury, Connecticut

An immigrant proudly displays a U.S. flag in the window of his diner in Connecticut.

Reading Consultant
Jeanne Clidas, Ph.D.
*National Reading Consultant
and Professor of Reading,
SUNY Brockport*

Content Consultant
Jonathan Riehl, J.D.
*Graduate Instructor,
Communication Studies
University of North Carolina,
Chapel Hill*

*The photograph on the cover
shows immigrants proudly
showing off their certificates of
naturalization after becoming
U.S. citizens. The photograph
on the title page shows people
waiting in line to file immigration papers at a U.S. Consulate
in Mexico.*

Library of Congress Cataloging-in-Publication Data

De Capua, Sarah.
    How people immigrate / by Sarah De Capua.
        p. cm. — (A true book)
    Summary: Explains what immigration is, who may immigrate to the
United States, what the process of immigration is, and how immigrants
get settled in their new nation.
    Includes bibliographical references and index.
    ISBN 0-516-22799-8 (lib. bdg.)   0-516-27940-8 (pbk.)
    1. United States—Emigration and immigration—Juvenile literature. [1.
United States—Emigration and immigration. 2. Immigrants—United
States.] I. Title. II. Series.
JV6465.D43 2003
325.73—dc22   2003012515

CHILDREN'S PRESS, and A TRUE BOOK™, and associated logos are
trademarks and or registered trademarks of Scholastic Library Publishing.
SCHOLASTIC and associated logos are trademarks and or registered
trademarks of Scholastic Inc.
1 2 3 4 5 6 7 8 9 10 R 13 12 11 10 09 08 07 06 05 04

Contents

What Is Immigration?

Do you know anyone who has come from another country to live in the United States? Perhaps you or your parents are immigrants. An immigrant is a person who was born in one country and leaves that country to live permanently in another. He or she goes through a process called immigration in order to call the new country home.

Most people in the United States have relatives or family members who were immi-grants. Throughout its history, the United States has been a place of freedom and oppor-tunity. People from all over the world who are seeking a better life for themselves and their families look to the United States.

Over the years, millions of immigrants have come to the United States in search of better lives. Here, European immigrants arrive in New York City in the early 1900s.

Immigrants arriving in the United States from Mexico

Today, more than 30 million immigrants live in the United States. The laws that govern their entry are overseen by the Bureau of Citizenship and Immigration Services (BCIS). This bureau is part of the U.S. Department of Homeland Security (DHS).

Immigrants and

People who enter the United States legally from other countries are divided into two categories: "nonimmigrants" and "immigrants." Nonimmigrants are those who want to come to the United States for a short stay—for vacation or business, to attend school, to seek medical care, or to work at a temporary job. They plan to

Nonimmigrants include people who are working (top) or studying (bottom) in the United States for a limited time.

Nonimmigrants

return to their home country. Nonimmigrants are issued temporary **visas**. These are documents giving them permission to enter and stay in the United States for a limited period of time.

Immigrants come to the United States to make this country their new, permanent home. Their goals include gaining the freedom and **prosperity** the United States has to offer. Immigrants are also called Lawful Permanent Residents. They are issued permanent visas giving them permission to live and work in the United States.

A Russian immigrant stands proudly in front of the store she opened after settling permanently in the United States.

Who Can Immigrate?

People from nearly every country in the world have come to live in the United States. Each year, the United States processes millions of immigration applications. However, not everyone who wants to immigrate gets permission to do so.

The U.S. government sets a limit each year on how many people may immigrate—in recent years, about 750,000. It offers only a certain number of immigrant visas each year to each country in the world. Also, most people must meet one of the following **qualifications** to have their requests for immigration approved:

- The person has a parent, **spouse**, brother or sister, or child over the age of twenty-one who is a U.S. **citizen** and can support him or her financially. This is called family-sponsored immigration.

- The person has a parent or spouse who is a Lawful Permanent Resident of the United States and can support him or her financially.

These Cuban children were allowed to immigrate to the United States to join their father, a doctor living in Miami, Florida.

- The person has been offered a job by a U.S. employer.

- The person is a professional (such as a surgeon) whose skills are needed in the United States.

Refugees from the war-torn country of Rwanda arrive at a U.S. airport.

- The person is a refugee. Refugees are people forced to leave their countries because of war, **persecution**, or natural disasters.

- The person is seeking **asylum**. People seeking asylum want to escape personal danger that exists in their home country.

A person may be denied permission to enter the United States for many reasons, including:

- The person has a **contagious** disease or a mental disorder that poses a threat to other people.

- The person engages in illegal or **terrorist** activities.

- The person is unable or unwilling to find work.

- The person has engaged in smuggling, or bringing goods into the country illegally.

- The person is trying to avoid performing military service in his or her home country.

People who are caught entering the United States illegally are sent back to their home country. These men were trying to cross the border by hiding in the trunk of a car.

- The person has been caught trying to enter the United States illegally, without going through the official immigration process.

- The person is a child kidnapper.

- The person has been previously deported, or ordered to leave the United States. A foreigner may be deported for a number of reasons, including entering the country illegally, engaging in criminal activity, or staying in the United States longer than his or her visa allows.

It is important to have rules that exclude some people from entering the country. Some people are dangerous. They may plan to come to the country to cause harm to others. These rules protect not only U.S. citizens, but honest immigrants, too.

Most immigrants respect the laws of their home country. They also respect the laws of the United States. They want to improve their lives and the lives of their families. In most cases, BCIS officials will determine that they meet the proper qualifications and allow them to immigrate.

A person whose application is approved will be issued a permanent visa and can immigrate as a Lawful Permanent Resident. He or she receives a Permanent

Resident Card, also known as a "green card." This identification card proves that the immigrant has permission to live and work in the United States. The card includes the person's name,

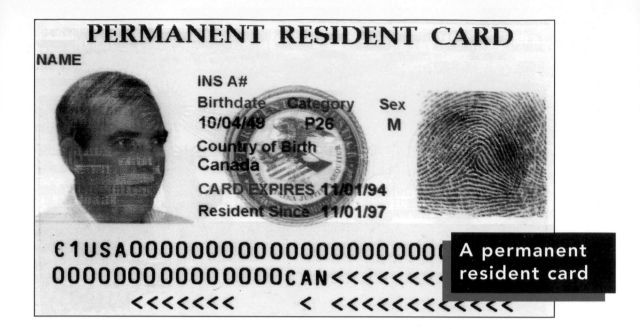

A permanent resident card

date of birth, photograph, and fingerprint. A registration number is also included. Immigrants must get a new Permanent Resident Card every ten years. Most, though, can apply for U.S. citizenship after five years if they wish to become U.S. citizens.

The Diversity Visa Lottery

Every year, fifty thousand lucky people win permission to immigrate to the United States through the U.S. State Department's Diversity Visa Lottery. It offers green cards to people from countries that have sent few immigrants to the United States in recent years. The lottery is not open to people from countries that have sent more than fifty thousand immigrants to the United States in the past five years.

A person must have at least a high-school education to qualify for the lottery. Those who are selected are also allowed to bring their spouses, as well as any unmarried children under the age of twenty-one, to the United States.

The government accepts mail-in applications for exactly one month. Each year, it receives more than ten million applications for the fifty thousand available green cards.

A woman from Bangladesh fills out the form for the Diversity Visa Lottery.

How Do People Immigrate?

Immigration is a long process. People in some countries have to wait for long periods before they can immigrate. In some countries, the wait is only a few months. In others, there are so many people who want to leave that the wait is several years.

Hong Kong residents line up outside Hong Kong's U.S. Consulate while waiting to fill out U.S. immigration forms.

The immigration process contains many different steps. It can be difficult to understand. It is important for an immigrant to follow the process so he or she will be a legal immigrant.

Legal immigrants receive official permission from U.S. immigration officials to live in the United States.

Most people who want to move to the United States begin at the U.S. Consulate in their home country. There they can find a lot of information about the types of visas that are available. They can also find out what types of immigration forms to fill out. This can be one of the most difficult parts

People seeking visas to the United States wait patiently at the U.S. Consulate in Ciudad Juarez, Mexico, the world's busiest immigrant visa post.

of the process. The United States has more than forty different immigration forms! Filing forms with the Department of Homeland Security costs money, so it is also important to find out the amounts. People who have Internet access can go to the DHS Website (www.dhs.gov) to find immigration rules, procedures, and forms.

It is important for a person to figure out what immigration category he or she belongs to, such as family member of a U.S. resident, student, or worker. Each category has a specific list of requirements that must be met in order to receive permission to enter the United States. If every requirement is not met, the person will not be allowed to come to the United States.

For example, if a foreign family member of a U.S. citizen or U.S. permanent resident wants to immigrate to the United States, a **petition** must be filed by a sponsor. A sponsor is a U.S. citizen or permanent resident who is a relative of the person who wants to immigrate.

After a six-year wait to join her husband in the United States, a woman and her family receive their visas.

The petition is filed at the sponsor's local immigration office.

The petition form must be filled out completely and honestly. Petition forms request information about the sponsor, including name, address, date of birth, and social security number (for U.S. citizens) or registration number (for permanent residents). The petition must include proof that the sponsor is a U.S. citizen or a permanent resident.

Proof that the sponsor and family member who wants to immigrate are related is also required. This may be a marriage certificate. If the family member is a child, a birth certificate issued in the foreign country is proof. Photographs are required too.

If U.S. immigration officers approve the petition, the next step is completing the application. The application must include the official notice that the petition was accepted. It also includes documents such as a passport, photographs, and the relative's fingerprints.

A woman has a photograph taken that will be used on her immigrant visa.

The sponsor and his or her relative must also be interviewed by immigration officials. This helps prove they are related. If the application is accepted

An immigration inspector prepares to stamp the passports of a family entering the United States.

and the interview is passed, the relative receives permission to enter the United States. The immigrant must enter the country within four months. When the immigrant arrives in the United States, an immigration official places a stamp in the person's passport. The stamp shows that the immigrant is a permanent resident.

A woman who came from China through family-sponsored immigration shows off her new temporary green card to her son-in-law and granddaughter.

Getting Settled

It can be challenging for an immigrant to enter the United States. Once that person has arrived, there are even more challenges ahead.

Understanding life in the United States can be particularly difficult for those immigrants who do not speak English. Some

Immigrants taking a class to learn English

immigrants take English classes
before or after they arrive in the
United States. Learning English
helps immigrants find jobs and
homes. It also helps them understand such things as rules for
driving and signs in grocery stores.

When they first arrive, immigrants may live for a time with family members already settled in the United States.

Some of the first issues facing immigrants are finding jobs and places to live. Many immigrants who join family members in the United States live with them for a time. They save money by working at a new job to buy or rent their own place to live.

Other issues facing newcomers to the United States include getting a driver's license, finding a doctor, enrolling children in school, and joining a house of worship. Nonimmigrants who drive in the United States are not required to obtain a U.S.

Many schools provide English classes for children of immigrants from non-English-speaking countries.

driver's license. Permanent residents who want to drive need a U.S. license to do so.

Many immigrants move to communities where a lot of people from their native country have settled. While adjusting to life in a new country, it can be helpful to live near others who speak the same native language and have been through the experience of immigration. Immigrants also appreciate what they can learn about everyday American life from American citizens.

It can be helpful for immigrants to find a community of people from their home country. Here, Sikh immigrants from India stand outside a Sikh temple in New Jersey.

The goal of most people who immigrate to the United States is naturalization—becoming a citizen. This is another long process. An immigrant must be in the country for a certain amount of

A man and woman are interviewed by an immigration official as part of the process of becoming U.S. citizens.

time before he or she can begin this process. Even so, many believe that the long process is worth it. Citizenship allows a person to take advantage of all the privileges guaranteed to U.S. citizens. These include voting, holding political office, and serving on a jury. Citizenship is the chance to fully take part in American society. After all, immigrants were the people who built this country into a place where so many of the world's people want to live.

People celebrate after taking part in a ceremony to become U.S. citizens.

To Find Out More

Here are some additional resources to help you learn more about immigration:

 **Books**

De Capua, Sarah. **Becoming a Citizen.** Children's Press, 2002.

De Capua, Sarah. **Making a Law.** Children's Press, 2004.

Freedman, Russell. **Immigrant Kids.** Penguin Putnam Books for Young Readers, 1995.

Wernick, Allan. **U.S. Immigration & Citizenship.** Prima Publishing, 2002.

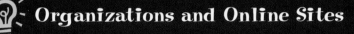

Organizations and Online Sites

American Immigration Center
http://www.us-immigration. com

This site includes information about immigration, becoming a citizen, and more.

Department of Homeland Security
http://www.dhs.gov

Check out this site for the latest information about immigration, border protection, and homeland safety.

Immigration and Refugee Services of America
http://www.irsa-uscr.org

This site includes up-to-date information and facts about immigration and U.S. citizenship.

National Immigration Forum
50 F Street NW, Suite 300
Washington, D.C. 20001
http://www. immigrationforum.org

At this site you can find the latest news and information about immigration and related issues.

Important Words

asylum protection given by a country to people escaping from danger in their own country

citizen member of a particular country who has certain rights, including voting and holding public office

contagious spread by direct contact

persecution cruel and unfair treatment because of a person's political or religious beliefs or ethnic background

petition document that asks people in power to grant something

prosperity financial success

qualifications conditions that make one able to do something

spouse husband or wife

terrorist referring to the use of violence to frighten people

visa document giving permission for someone to enter a foreign country

Index

Meet the Author

Sarah De Capua works as an editor and author of children's books. As the author of many nonfiction works, she enjoys educating children through her books. Other titles she has written in the True Books series include *Becoming a Citizen, Being a Governor, Making a Law, Paying Taxes, Running for Public Office, Serving on a Jury,* and *Voting.*

Born and raised in Connecticut, Ms. De Capua currently resides in Colorado.